SLAM, Project Pluto and the Uninhabited Nuclear Powered Bomber

HUGH HARKINS

SLAM, Project Pluto and the Uninhabited Nuclear Powered Bomber

© Hugh Harkins 2019

Centurion Publishing
United Kingdom

ISBN 10: 1-903630-50-9
ISBN 13: 978-1-903630-50-1

This volume first published in 2019

Cover design © Centurion Publishing and KDP
Page layout, concept and design © Centurion Publishing

The author and publisher would like to thank all organisations and services for their assistance and contributions in the preparation of this volume

CONTENTS

INTRODUCTION

In 2018, the Russian Federation unveiled the Burevestnik (Petrel) cruise missile, which, in order to achieve its global range to facilitate the mission requirement of circumventing modern missile defence systems, employs a small nuclear reactor for propulsion. The concept of installing a nuclear reactor in a cruise missile or uninhabited strike vehicle had been around since the mid-twentieth century when United States and Soviet Union designers worked on such vehicles in an attempt to field viable nuclear deterrent carrying air vehicles to supplement and potentially replace crewed strategic bombers.

Conceived in the late 1950's as a Mach 3+ global range nuclear warhead delivery system, the Chance Vought SLAM (Supersonic Low Altitude Missile), powered by a ramjet engine propelled by a nuclear reactor developed under Project Pluto, can be considered an unrealised anachronism of the Cold War era. This was a period when human kind proved its ingenuity in many fields, including, unfortunately, that of provisioning the ability to destroy itself on an ever increasing scale.

This volume looks at the genesis and development of the SLAM concept, the results of Project Pluto and details how the concept lost out to the intercontinental ballistic missile concept as the major delivery system for nuclear weapons in the 1960's. The volume is supported by photographs, technical drawings, renderings and flight vehicle and nuclear propulsion planned performance charts. All technical data relating to the concepts have been supplied by contractors and test organisations.

There is a deliberate switch from imperial measurements/weights to the fore and metric measurements/weights secondary to metric to the fore and imperial secondary at various stages in the text. This has been done to ensure 100% accuracy in primary reporting from respective designer/test/research organisations, whereas secondary data on measurements/weights may, at times, be rounded to the nearest cm, kg, inch or lb.

SLAM, PROJECT PLUTO AND THE UNINHABITED NUCLEAR POWERED BOMBER

The 1950's and 1960's were a time of accelerated research and development in many fields of aeronautics, including that of intercontinental strike platforms, in both power blocs of East and West, locked in a nuclear stand-off universally referred to as the Cold War. There were plans for nuclear powered inhabited strategic bomber aircraft and later nuclear powered spacecraft – some of these space vehicles would be brought to fruition, just as the nuclear powered submarine and surface ships had been developed from the 1950's and continue to be developed in many forms in the twenty first century. Fate has not shone so favourably on the nuclear powered aircraft concept, inhabited or uninhabited (for the purposes of this volume, uninhabited aircraft or air vehicle will generally refer to the cruise missile concept).

The US (United States) Chance Vought SLAM (Supersonic Low Altitude Missile) concept called for an uninhabited nuclear powered strike air vehicle capable of flying at multi-Mach speeds to strike multiple targets in the USSR (Union of Soviet Socialist Republics – Soviet Union) with free fall atomic bombs. The idea of pilotless missiles, or warhead delivery vehicles, was not new. There were a number of programs in a number of countries in the first half of the twentieth century, but it was the German V-1 concept that proved the ground launched cruise missile as a viable strike weapon in the last year of World War II (1944-1945). However, the effectiveness of this weapon was handicapped by poor accuracy and limited warhead power. The V-1 concept would be tested and further developed by the Soviet Union (FAU-1) and United States (JB-2 Loon) in the immediate post-war years – the second half of the 1940's. Experience gained on such programs would feed into development of more advanced weapons with longer range. In the United States these designs included the Martin B-61 (TM-61A) Matador and it's replacement, the Marin TM-76 Mace, developed as surface launched missiles with ranges under 1,000 miles (~1609 km). Range and maximum speed of the TM-61 was 690 miles (~1110 km) and 600 mph (~966 km/h) respectively, limiting the target sets the weapon could be employed against and rendering it vulnerable to defensive countermeasures.

The first launch was conducted in January 1949 and TM-61 missiles were delivered, for training purposes, to the USAF (United States Air Force) first Pilotless Bomber Squadron (Light) in October 1951. The first operational unit equipped with the TM-61 was deployed to West Germany in March 1954, in excess of 1,000 such missiles being delivered to USAF units by summer 1957. Phase out commenced in 1959 (NMUSAF).

Top: A 1/10-scale model of the Chance Vought Supersonic Low Altitude Missile uninhabited nuclear powered strategic strike complex of the early 1960's. Above: B-61 (TM-61) Matador surface launched cruise missile. VHC/NMUSAF

The CGM-13B (initially the vehicle was designated TM-76 and then MGM-13) Mace increased range and flight speed moderately over than attained by the TM-61A, but the subsonic speed rendered Mace vulnerable to Soviet surface to air and fighter defences, as had been the case for the Matador. Development of Mace had commenced in 1954 and the first launch was conducted in 1956. The CGM-13A remained in service until the mid-1960's, by which time the CGM-13B, which extended range out to 1400 miles (~2253 km) on a high altitude attack profile, reducing to 585 nm (~1083 km) on a low altitude attack profile (CGM-13B CS, 1969) with a cruise speed of 650 mph was in service. Development of this variant had commenced in 1959, service entry was attained in 1961 and the weapon system remained in service until the early 1970's. As had been the case with the Matador and 'A' Model Mace, the CGM-13B was vulnerable to Soviet surface to air and air defence fighter defence systems (NMUSAF & CGM-13B CS, 1963).

The drive to introduce an uninhabited platform capable of performing a strategic strike mission led to the development of the Northrop SM-62A Snark. Design of the guidance system was initiated in March 1946, design of the XSSM-A-3 flight vehicle commenced in January 1947 and the XASSM-A-3A (N-69E) in June 1950. The XSSM-A-3 conducted its maiden flight in March 1951 and the XASSM-A-3A, on slightly different production method XSM-62 (N-72) form, conducted its maiden flight in August 1953. Category 1 testing ended in September 1958 and the first production example was delivered to the USAF Strategic Air Command in June 1959 and entered service in March 1960 (SM-62A CS, 1960 & SM-62A SAC, 1960).

SM-62 Snark surface launched cruise missile in flight. Missile characteristics included: Length, 69.9 ft.; span: 42.3 ft. and height, 14.8 ft. NMUSAF

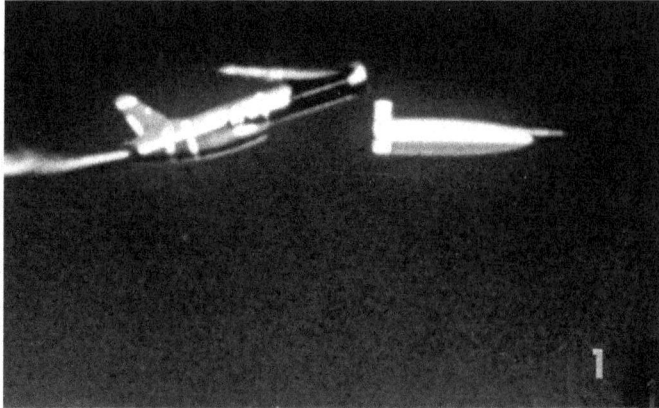

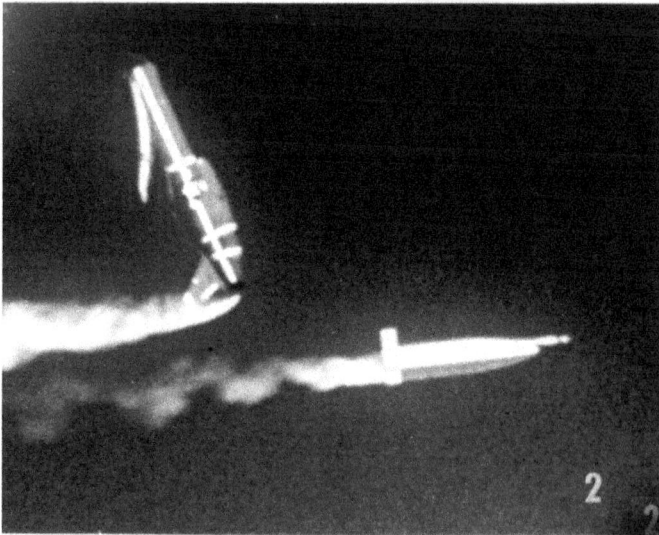

SM-62 Snark nose section with the warhead separating from the missile body at engine cut-off, before continuing its descent toward the target area. NMUSAF

The SM-62 was powered by a Pratt & Whitney J57-P-17 turbojet, rated at 10,500 lb. (~4763 kg) in military power, and an Allegany Ballistics Laboratory X-226-A3 Solid Rocket booster, rated at 130,000 lb. (58967 kg), with a 4 second run time. Launch weight of the missile, which was launched from a mobile short-rail launch complex, was up to 60,968 lb. (~27655 kg) and the missile had a range out to 5,322 nm (~9856 km), depending on flight profile and configuration. After a sea level launch the missile climbed to 32,000 ft. (~9754 m) to commence the cruise phase of the flight, which continued the climb to 44,650 ft. (~13609 m) at the end of the cruise phase, with a further climb to 50,900 ft. (~15514 m) altitude over the target area for the warhead ballistic release, at which point speed was 540 knots (~621.4 mph/~1000 km/h) (SM-62A CS, 1960).

The subsonic speed of the SM-62 rendered the system vulnerable to the first generation ZRS S-25 Berkut Soviet SAM (Surface to Air Missile) intended to defend against strategic strike platforms. The first successful launch of a Model-205 SAM occurred on 2 November 1952, and on 25 April 1953, the system hit a Tupolev Tu-4 target bomber at an altitude of 7000 m (~22,965 ft.) (PJSC NPO Almaz & Laspace). The initial S-25 standard, introduced to operational service in 1955, was capable of intercepting bombers flying at speeds up to 1500 km/h (~932 mph) at altitudes up to 20 km (65,616 ft.) at slant ranges out to 35 km (~22 miles) (PJSC NPO Almaz), well within the operational envelope of the SM-62A.

To address the vulnerability to Soviet air defence systems inherent in the SM-62A design the United States commenced development of a multi-Mach nuclear payload delivery system, which would evolve into the North American SM-64 Navaho design, developed under the WS-104A program, which aimed to field a strategic strike platform with a range out to 5500 nm (10186 km). The XSM-64A detail design was released in December 1954. The design had a combined delivery vehicle and booster launch weight of 290,000 lb. (131542 kg), which included a 7,000 lb. (~3175 kg) allowance for the payload. Power was supplied by 2 x Wright Aerospace Corporation XRJ47-W-7 turbojet engines, each rated at 20,070 lb. (~9104 kg) at 45,000 ft. (13716 m) altitude. The range projection was 5500 nm (10186 km) at a cruise speed of 1868 knots (Mach 3.25). Following surface launch from the vertical launcher erected on a concrete launch pad the missile would climb to 70,000 ft. (21336 m) for booster separation, following which the missile would drop in altitude and climbed several times until altitude was 57,500 ft. (17526 m) where the cruise flight commenced to the target proximity, which was to be reached with the missile at an altitude of 82,900 ft. (~25267 m). The missile would now climb to 90,300 ft. (~27524 m) and conducted a more or less vertical dive to the target. Planned accuracy was poor, with an estimated 50% of impacts expected to be within 2 nm (~3.70 km) of the target. Guidance was inertial and the missile was controlled by auto-navigation and auto-pilot complexes. Alternate warheads would have included a 3,000 lb. (~1361 kg) or 15,000 lb. (~6804 kg) special (nuclear) store (SM-64A CS, 1957 & SM-64A SAC, 1957), the latter would have resulted in reduced fuel carriage or increased weight, with a corresponding reduction in range.

In the age of the ICBM (Intercontinental Ballistic Missile) the SM-64 design was rendered obsolete in that the up to 16 plus hours was required to prepare the missile for launch, which translated to increased risk that the launch facility could be knocked out by a ballistic missile strike before the SM-64 could be made ready for use. The SM-64 would also have been vulnerable to advancements in Soviet air defence capability – by 1966, the modernised S-25 Berkut system was capable of intercepting bombers and missiles flying at speeds up to 4200 km/h (2,610 mph/(~Mach 3.4)) at altitudes up to 30 km (~98,425 ft.) and slant ranges out to 43.4 km (~27 miles) (PJSC NPO Almaz). The ICBM was emerging as a more survivable nuclear payload delivery vehicle, able to strike targets at longer range and higher speeds than that planned for the SM-64, and with a much higher degree of immunity from Soviet countermeasures. The SM-64 vulnerability to air defences, combined with the development potential of the ICBM, led to the programs cancellation in 1957 (NMUSAF).

Development of an uninhabited intercontinental airborne strike platform was also underway in the Soviet Union in the 1950's. This was conducted under a Resolution of the USSR Council dated 20 May 1954. This authorised studies that would lead to the MSCS Storm (Tempest) CRMD Intercontinental Supersonic Cruise Missile, developed by OKB-301 (S.A. Lavochkin) in a competition that included the OKB-23 V.M. Myasishchev Buran intercontinental cruise missile concept. The Storm (Tempest) concept, which was developed through to flight test, had a launch weight of 95000 kg (~209,439 lb.) for the missile and 33000 kg (~72,752 lb.) for the sustainer sections. The vehicle was intended to attain a speed of Mach 3.2, an upper cruise altitude of 25 km (~82,025 ft.) and a flight range of 8000 km (~4971 miles) (Laspace).

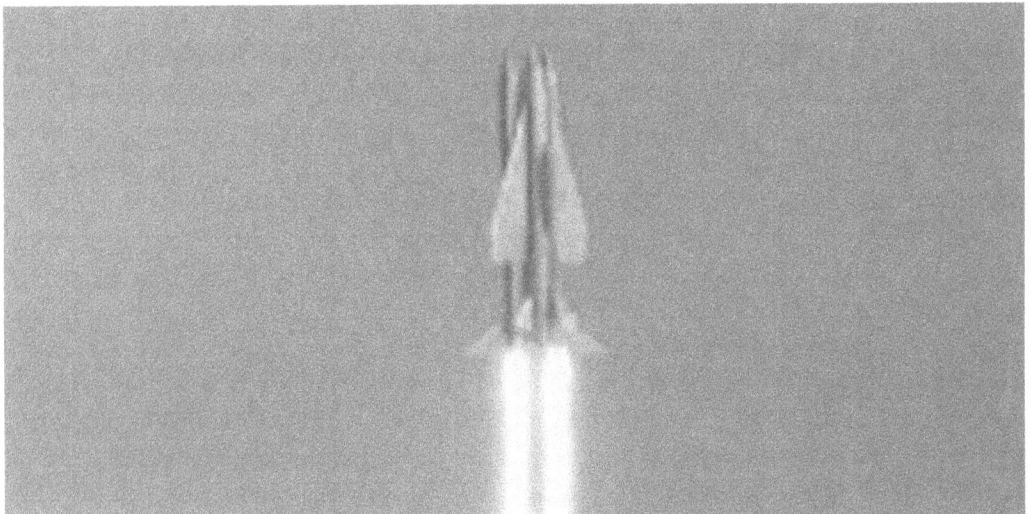

Flight test of the Lavochkin Storm (Tempest) Intercontinental Supersonic Cruise Missile. Laspace

Flight testing commenced on 31 July 1957. The first full launch took place on 1 September 1957, but the first fully successful launch did not take place until 22 May 1958 (fifth launch). A total of 19 Tempest missiles were built, 17 of which were launched. The final launch, on 16 December 1960, resulted in the missile flying 6500 km (~4038 miles). During the limited flight test phase the Tempest attained a cruise speed of 3500 km/h (~2,175 mph) before program cancellation ceased further envelope expansion flights (Laspace).

No SM-64 Navaho missiles were built, but the North American X-10 was developed to test a number of SM-64 characteristics and the guidance, navigation and flight control systems planned for the Navaho. The first X-10, powered by two Westinghouse XJ40 turbojet engines, each rated at 10,000 lb. (~4536 kg) thrust with afterburner, conducted its maiden flight in October 1953. Thirteen X-10 vehicles were built, ten of which were flown, several being destroyed during tests in support of the Navaho program. The X-10 had a design maximum speed of 1,300 mph (~2092 km/h), range was 400 miles (~644 km) and ceiling was 45,000 ft. (10668 m) A maximum speed of Mach 2.05 had been attained with the X-10 program by the time the SM-64A program was cancelled (NMUSAF).

Officially the development of ICBM's was portrayed as the reason for the SM-64A demise. However, regardless of the development of ballistic missiles capable of delivering a warhead to targets at intercontinental range, the writing had been on the wall for the SM-64A program since the issuing of USAF System Requirement 149 (SR 149) in October 1956. This had called for studies of a winged missile configuration powered by a ramjet engine propelled by a nuclear reactor. Such a concept offered the advantage of unlimited range compared with a vehicle in the class of the SM-64A. In a similar timeframe, OKB-301 in the Soviet Union was conducting preliminary design work on a nuclear fueled ramjet (designer, M.M. Bondaryuk) powered missile designated 375, but this work was cancelled due to the rise in prominence of the first generation R-7 ICBM (Laspace).

North American X-10 flight vehicle on display at the NMUSAF. The X-10 was employed in support of the SM-64A program. NMUSAF

In the United States, studies into the use of nuclear energy for vehicle propulsion had commenced in New York in May 1946. The program was moved to Oak Ridge National Laboratory, Oak Ridge, Tennessee, in September than year. The overall nuclear propulsion for aircraft effort was conducted under the supervision of NEPA (Nuclear Energy for Propulsion of Aircraft), the US AEC (Atomic Energy Commission) commencing such under the overall USAF NEPA program, at Oak Ridge in autumn 1949. A major effort was conducted into studies of direct air cycle concepts. This would involve air being heated through conduction when it transited through the reactor (RMANPP AEC, 1963 & VHC).

Development of ceramic reactors had been a breakthrough in the development road to the design of a nuclear ramjet engine, which, it was hoped, would bestow a global range upon a future uninhabited aircraft (cruise missile) weapon system. The US Office of Strategic Development had requested, in November 1955, that the Atomic Energy Commission should conduct a feasibility study of the nuclear ramjet concept, this sowing the seeds that would germinate into Project Pluto. While Project Pluto was concerned with nuclear propulsion research for ramjet equipped uninhabited aircraft/missiles the nuclear propulsion of rockets was to be conducted under Project Rover, Project Snap was concerned with research into various systems for nuclear auxiliary power, and NEPA was concerned with studying the viability of inhabited aircraft propelled by a nuclear fueled power plant (RMANPP AEC, 1963).

Initial proposals for a nuclear powered air vehicle predominantly focused on inhabited platforms. In April 1955, following the issuing of a RFP (Request for Proposals) to six aircraft companies a series of fixed price contracts were awarded by the USAF for studies into a nuclear powered strategic bombardment weapon system. The contract recipients were Convair (Contract No. AF 33(600)-30292), Lockheed (AF 33-(600)-30293) and Boeing Airplane Company (AF 33-(600)-30291) – these three contract recipients being the only ones to respond to the RFP. The contracts were considered a step toward future development contracts for Weapon System 125A. Boeing was dropped from what had become the ANP (Aircraft Nuclear Propulsion) program as it was involved in the Weapon System 110A competition to field a chemical fueled strategic bomber platform, having studied a number of strategic bomber concepts, including MX-2145. Further contracts were awarded to Convair (AF 33(038)-21117) and Lockheed (AF (038)-21118), which would effectively tie up airframe and engine contractors (Convair with GE (General Electric) and Lockheed with P&W (Pratt & Whitney). Extensions to these contracts were awarded to Convair (AF 33(600)-32054) and Lockheed (AF 33(600)-32055) and definitive contracts were awarded in April 1956 and May 1957 to Convair and Lockheed respectively. These contracts provisioned for development of a strategic strike aircraft capable of cruise under nuclear propulsion, which would be augmented by chemical fuel propulsion during the penetration phase of the missions in order to increase performance – development aircraft were to be built as prototypes for what were termed CAML (Continuously Airborne Missile Launcher), which would operate at altitudes of around 40,000-50,000 ft. (12192-15240 m) and the CAMAL (Continuous Airborne Missile Launcher and Low Level Weapon) weapon system. The contracts were altered to fixed price contracts in September 1958. The design competition, calling for a single contractor to be selected to produce both aircraft designs, saw Convair being selected to go forward to the prototype stage with the award of contract AF 33(600)-38964 on 30 March 1959. Both designs were eventually rejected by the USAF, but Convair was awarded contract AF 33(600)-38946, which partnered it with GE to develop a prototype for a nuclear powered strategic bomber – this design would take on characteristics of the Convair Model 54, which was itself evolved from the now defunct Convair CAMAL design. By October 1960, the program concentrated on the NX-2 design, which was evolved from the Model 54. This design was to be tasked with demonstrating the operation of nuclear fueled power plants employing either direct or indirect cycle design. Through a few more twists and turns the ANP program was eventually terminated in March 1961 (RMANPP AEC, 1963).

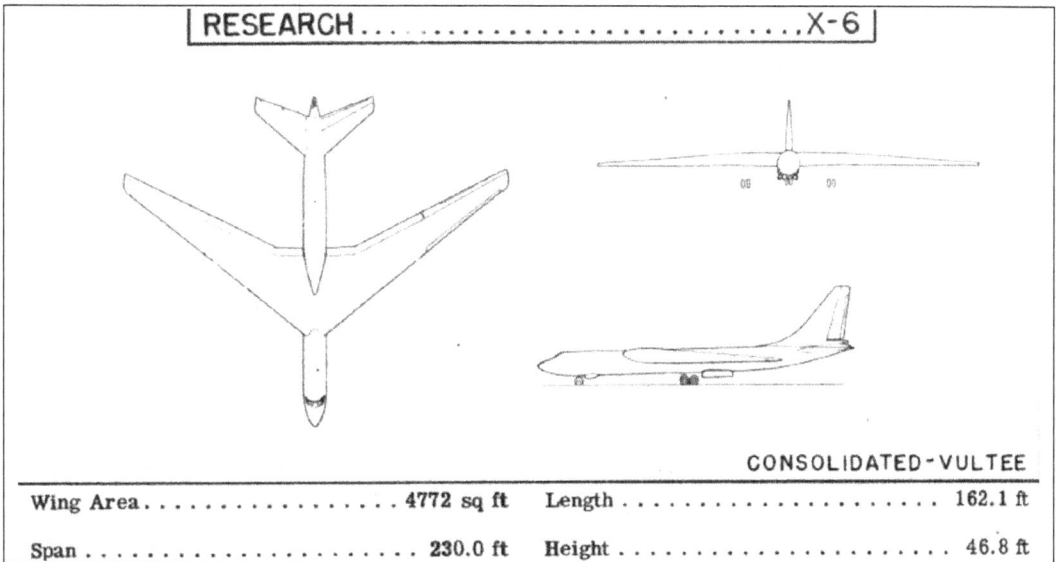

RESEARCH . . . . , X-6

CONSOLIDATED-VULTEE

Wing Area . . . . 4772 sq ft	Length . . . . 162.1 ft
Span . . . . 230.0 ft	Height . . . . 46.8 ft

Top: The Convair NB-36H Crusader in flight. This aircraft retained the B-36H piston/turbojet power plant and carried an operable nuclear reactor in the aircraft rear section. Above: The scheme for the Convair X-6 aircraft designed to test a nuclear power plant for a manned bomber. NMUSAF/X-6 CS, 1952 (August)

While the nuclear powered strategic bombardment designs were destined to remain unbuilt concept programs, a shielded nuclear reactor was taken aloft in the Convair NB-36H 'Crusader'. This aircraft, converted from a damaged B-36H-20-CF strategic bomber, serial 51-5712, was developed not as a nuclear propulsion test bed, but rather as a conventional powered – piston/turbojet combination of the B-36H strategic bomber – airborne platform to carry a nuclear reactor payload aloft to garner data on the unknowns of the reaction process and shielding research, which would be carried over to the planned X-6 program. In NB-36H configuration the aircraft flew 47 times during 1955-1957 (NMUSAF).

The Convair X-6 was a development of the B-36 strategic bomber that would be designed from the outset to test a nuclear reactor power plant in-flight. A letter contract was awarded on 17 February 1951, a definitive contract was awarded on 18 September 1952 and the prototype first flight was scheduled for December 1956 (November 1952 estimate) (X-6 CS, 1952a). The program was terminated, work being concluded between April-June 1953 (RMANPP AEC, 1963), as the future of manned strategic bomber design focused on chemical fueled engine designs.

EARLY NUCLEAR PROPELLED RAMJET STUDIES

While Weapon System 125A (nuclear fueled strategic strike aircraft) and Weapon System 110A (chemical fueled strategic bomber) were progressing, the USAF was also looking at the viability of an uninhabited nuclear strike platform. The two main areas to be investigated were ballistic missiles and air breathing cruise missiles – both chemical fueled and nuclear fueled concepts were to be investigated. Although the inhabited nuclear propelled airborne strategic strike platform had fallen by the wayside, development of an uninhabited nuclear propelled airborne strategic strike platform continued, alongside development of an operable nuclear reactor under Project Pluto. Predating Project Pluto, NACA (National Advisory Committee for Aeronautics) conducted studies on 'direct-air, shieldless [no heavy shielding against the radioactive effects of the fissionable gamma rays and neutrons], nuclear-powered, ram-jet missile' feasibility in the first half of the 1950's (Rom, 1954). These studies fell on what was described as a nuclear reactor that utilised BO (Beryllium Oxide) for moderation and was 'cooled by air flowing through smooth reactor passages' (Rom, 1954 & VHC).

The major drawback of the theoretical nuclear propulsion for air vehicles was identified as the heavy weight of the shielding that was necessary to protect the crew from the damaging effects of radiation. Such heavy shielding required that the aircraft had to be of large mass, requiring even more power as a result. It was considered that the weight of the shielding could be reduced if the diameter of the reactor was itself reduced. Removing the need for shielding would allow the power requirements to be reduced, with the knock on effect of easing the problem of heat-transfer from the high temperatures generated within the reactor. A shielded reactor employed for powering a large size aircraft would inevitably entail heightened thermal -transfer problems compared to a smaller reactor within a smaller air vehicle that did not require shielding (Sams & Rom, 1953 & Rom, 1954).

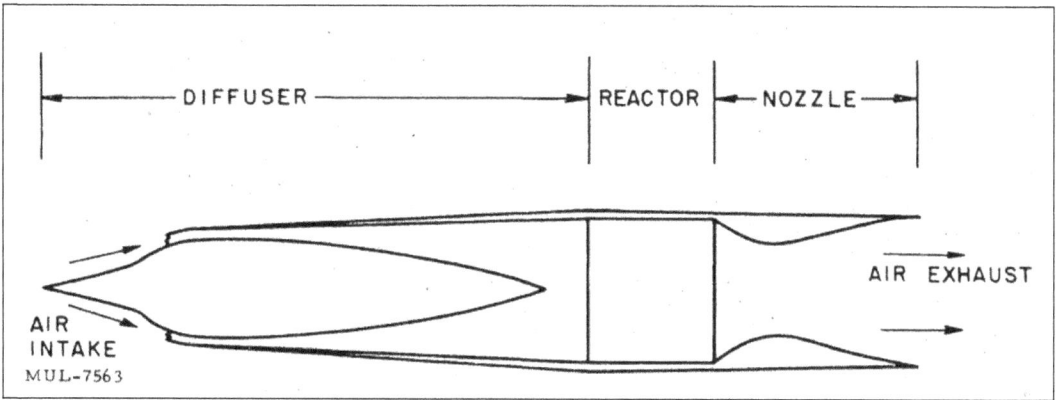

Conceptual arrangement of a nuclear ramjet c. early 1950's. Merkle, 1959

While the early studies showed that nuclear propulsion was more suitable for a small air vehicle such as a cruise missile, it was clear that such uninhabited designs posed their own set of problems not encountered in an inhabited aircraft design. Most critical of these, in regard to the ability of the vehicle to be employed as a viable weapon system, was that the uninhabited vehicle had to be remotely guided. Other negative impacts on such a design were that the electronics and sensors, including the above mentioned remote guidance system, had to be durable enough to withstand the damaging effects from radiation from the unshielded reactor and that the smaller uninhabited vehicle would have to be disposable at the end of the mission. This disposal would either by through impact in the target area for a single warhead missile or after jettisoning the last of the payload weapons in a multi-warhead carrying vehicle. This translated to the loss of the fissionable material within the reactor for a single mission. Financially it was considered that the loss of the fissionable material would be counterbalanced by the reduced unit costs of the uninhabited vehicle over that of large inhabited aircraft, the costs of which would have been prohibitive in comparison to the smaller missile. These costs concerned not only the production values, but also the cost of extensive ground maintenance and infrastructure required for the multi-use large inhabited aircraft (Rom, 1954). At the time it was not fully understood how damaging the ejection of fissionable material into the atmosphere would be, therefore, this was not stated as a great consideration in contemporary reports.

It was assumed that such a missile, as studied in 1954, would be launched from a fixed surface complex through the use of chemical fueled booster rockets, which would propel the missile to a pre-determined altitude and flight speed before the nuclear ramjet propulsion took over for the cruise flight phase. If the reactor was to be made critical before launch then it would have to be conducted in a remote location. If the launch facility was not that remote then criticality of the reactor would have to be accomplished automatically at the end of the boost phase, perhaps once the booster rocket(s) had been discarded. Air launching the nuclear powered missile from a chemical fuel powered large carrier aircraft was studied. In this guise it was considered that the reactor would, considering its lack of shielding, be made inoperative during its carriage on the carrier aircraft. The ramjet missile would be released from the carrier aircraft, following which it would accelerate under chemical fuel booster rocket power to cruise flight speed and altitude, at which point the reactor would automatically become operational (Rom, 1954).

The basic concept for the reactor/ramjet was considered to be relatively conventional with the major difference being that the reactor would heat the air entering the ramjet rather than a chemical fuel provided in a conventional fuel/ramjet configuration (Rom, 1954). The results of the studies included the finding that for a missile with a 10,000 lb. (~4536 kg) payload (includes electronics and sensors) capable of flying at Mach 2.5 at 50,000 ft. (15240 m) altitude, 19 lb. (~8.61 kg) of uranium would be required, reactor wall temperature value being 2200° R (total temperature), for a missile with a gross weight of 47,000 lb. (~21319 kg). This would rise to 20.6 lb. (~9.244 kg) of uranium, reactor wall temperature of 2000° R, for a missile with a gross weight of 44,300 lb. (~20094 kg) and a reactor wall temperature of 2200° R for a missile with a gross weight of 34,800 lb. (~15785 kg). A further increase to 23.6 lb. (~10.70 kg) of uranium would be required for a reactor wall temperature of 1800° R at a missile gross weight of 54,400 lb. (~24675 kg), a reactor wall temperature of 2000° R for a missile with a gross weight of 32,100 lb. (14515 kg) and a reactor wall temperature of 2200° R for a missile with a gross weight of 29,100 lb. (~13154 kg). Uranium weight increased to 25 lb. (~11.33 kg) for a reactor wall temperature of 1800° R at a missile gross weight of 39,500 lb. (~17917 kg), a reactor wall temperature of 2000° R for a missile with a gross weight of 30,400 lb. (~13789 kg) and a reactor wall temperature of 2200° R for a missile with a gross weight of 28,000 lb. (~12700 kg). The final category studied showed a requirement for 30 lb. (~13.6 kg) of uranium for a reactor wall temperature of 1800° R at a missile gross weight of 31,500 lb. (~14288 kg) and a reactor wall temperature of 2000° R for a missile with a gross weight of 27,500 lb. (~12473 kg) and a reactor wall temperature of 2200° R for a missile with a gross weight of 26,000 lb. (~11793 kg) (Lewis Flight Propulsion Lab, 1954 & Rom, 1954).

An earlier study, outlined in a 1953 report, showed that a missile with a gross weight of 64,000 lb. (~29029 kg), including a 10,000 lb. (~4536 kg) payload, operating at a speed of Mach 3.0 and an altitude of 70,000 ft. (21336 m), would require 81 lb. (~31.74 kg) uranium for the reactor (Sams & Rom, 1953). The conclusions of the early studies showed that a flight altitude of 50,000-70,000 ft. (15240-21336 m) and a flight speed of Mach 2.5 for a missile with a gross weight of 32,100 lb. (~14515 kg) required an investment (hot clean core) of 29.9 lb. (~13.56 kg) of uranium, with a reactor free flow ratio of 0.45 at a reactor inlet air Mach number of 0.30. At the same speed and altitude conditions, but with a gross weight of 45,400 lb. (~20593 kg), uranium investment (hot clean core) was 46.2 lb. (~20.96 kg), with a reactor free flow ratio of 0.52 at a reactor inlet air Mach number of 0.28. At the same altitude and speed conditions, but with a missile gross weight of 82,400 lb. (~37376 kg), uranium investment (hot clean core) was estimated at 222 lb. (~100.7 kg) of uranium, with reactor free flow ratio of 0.57 at a reactor inlet air Mach number of 0.30. For a flight altitude of 60,000 ft. (18288 m) at a flight speed of Mach 3, a missile with a gross weight of 82,400 lb.(37376 kg) required a uranium investment (hot clean core) estimated at 34.6 lb. (~15.7 kg) with a reactor free flow ratio of 0.50 at a reactor inlet air Mach number of 0.28. For a missile with a gross weight of 63,700 lb. (~28894 kg) at an altitude of 70,000 ft. (21336 m) and a speed of Mach 3.0, uranium investment (hot clean core) was estimated at 34.6 lb. with reactor free flow ratio of 0.59 at a reactor inlet air Mach number of 0.28 (Sams & Rom, 1953).

Missile speed, Mach	2.5	3.0
Flight altitude, ft.	50,000-70,000	60,000*-70,000
Reactor effective wall temperature, ° R	1800	1800
Reactor outlet-air temperature, ° R	Choke value minus 90°- - - - - - - - - - - - -	
Payload, lb.	10,000	10,000

*Calculations were also made for an altitude of 80,000 ft. (24384 m) at a flight speed of Mach 3.0. In order to obtain a viable missile at these conditions, the effective wall temperature would have had to have been considerably greater than 1800° R; hence, results for this case are not presented in the table

Table 1. Hypothetical characteristics of reactor performance as the propulsion for a hypothetical ground launched cruise missile. Data taken from Sams & Rom, 1953

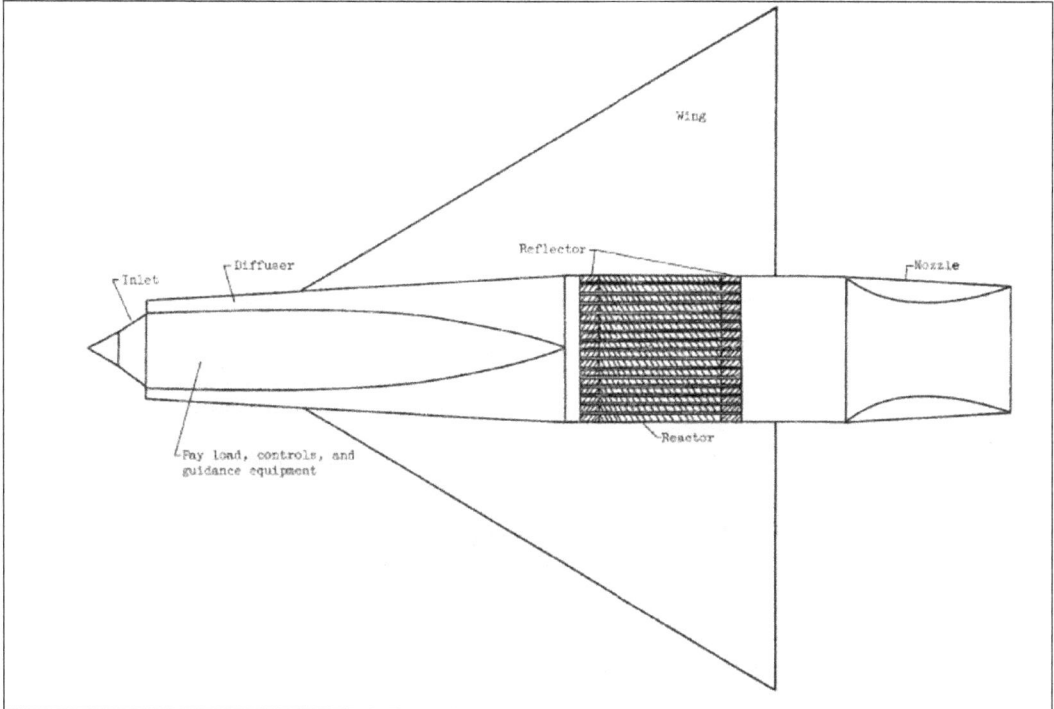

Diagram, dating to c 1953, of a hypothetical nuclear powered ramjet missile without shielding. NACA (NASA)

So interlocked were the inhabited and uninhabited elements of the ANP programs that no less than three of the five branches of ANPO (Aircraft Nuclear Propulsion Office) were organised to support both inhabited and uninhabited programs. While the Aircraft Projects Branch had responsibility for inhabited programs the Missile Projects Branch was responsible for current and proposed future concept formulation for uninhabited nuclear powered aircraft (cruise missiles) (RMNAPP AEC, 1963).

In October 1956, SR 149 (System Requirement 149) was issued by the USAF. This called for development of a winged missile capable of supersonic speeds in cruise flight. This was done in concert with concept studies for a reactor complex for an uninhabited aircraft (missile) under the NEPA project, this being conducted at General Electric's ANPP (Aircraft Nuclear Propulsion Project). As confidence in the viability of a ramjet powered by nuclear energy increased, the program was moved, in 1957, to LRL (Lawrence Radiation Laboratory), University of California. The combined design concept studies conducted indicated that a nuclear propulsion system for incorporation into an uninhabited aircraft (winged missile) was viable. The workings for the ramjet, in cooperation with Chance Vought's concept design for the winged missile vehicle, led to the design of a reactor concept with the characteristics outlined in Table 2 (VHC).

Diameter: 57.25 in
Fissionable core: 47.24 in
Length: 64.24 in
Core length: 50.70 in
Critical mass of uranium: 59.90 kg
Average power density: 10 MW/cubic foot
Total power: 600 MW
Average element temperature: 2,330° F

Table 2: SLAM vehicle concept nuclear reactor characteristics. Vought History Centre

Chance Vought's first foray into guided missile development was the PA-6 tactical missile, which was air launched from the Chance Vought F4U Corsair piston engine fighter aircraft. This short range weapon (around several hundred miles) was a world apart from the global range specified for the SLAM concept. VHC

This image is thought to show a reactor core being assembled in an oven facility. It is unclear if this is for the Tory IIA or Tory IIC reactor of Project Pluto, but given that the photo dates from 1959 or prior, it can be assumed that, if it was indeed associated with the Tory programs, then it is probably the Tory IIA. Merkle, 1959

In regard to design of the airframe for the uninhabited nuclear powered aircraft concept, Change-Vought, with no official state funding, put together a study group, headed by a Dr. Walt Hesse, in 1957. These studies, which were conducted simultaneously with studies conducted at several other aircraft design companies, led to the issuing to the aviation industry of a USAF Request for Proposals (VHC). In August 1958, three contractors – Convair, North American Aviation and Chance Vought – were selected to proceed to the USAF funded concept design phase for a nuclear powered cruise missile for strategic strike against targets at global range – mission parameters that no projected chemical fuel ramjet powered cruise missile was envisioned to be capable of replicating. A further competition, in early 1961, resulted in Chance Vought being selected to proceed to a demonstration study phase for a nuclear-powered winged missile concept, and sub-systems for same that would lead to the Supersonic Low Altitude Missile (SLAM) design. A contract was awarded to Chance Vought in April 1961 for the 'Aerothermo-dynamics for Pluto' – Pluto, of course, referring to the code name allocated to the research & development program that resulted in development of the ceramic nuclear reactor for the air vehicle (VHC).

In 1957 the US Atomic Energy Commission had forwarded a request to the Lawrence Radiation Laboratory for the latter to undertake development of a nuclear reactor for a ramjet powered air vehicle. A series of studies were undertaken to determine what category of air vehicle such a power plant would be suitable, for, emphasis eventually falling on a vehicle capable of supersonic speed (Goldberg, 1962). The vehicle would be propelled by thrust created through admission of ambient air through the air intake. This air would be heated to high temperatures as it passed through the reactor before being ejected through the engine exhaust nozzle. To test the viability of the reactor to power the ramjet and to determine the feasibility of the generation of the high thrust required to achieve multi-Mach speeds while carrying a reasonable payload of atomic warhead(s), a series of ground based test reactors were developed and run at reduced scale – Tory-IIA – and full-scale – Tory-IIC – under the auspices of Project Pluto (Goldberg, 1962 & VHC).

Development of the Pluto test site at the Atomic Energy Commissions facility at Jackass Flats, Nevada, referred to as the NTS (Nevada Test Site), had been initiated to provision for testing of the Tory I ground based Rover type reactor testbed for ballistic missiles. While the site was being developed, its role was changed from that of testing a Rover type reactor to that of testing Pluto type reactors that would emerge as the Tory IIA and Tory IIC reactors for the uninhabited nuclear propelled aircraft (cruise missile). As developed, the test site covered an area of around 8 square miles, within which was located the three main areas – control, disassembly and the test area, the disassembly area and the test bunker being linked by a railroad (PNPC, 1962 & Barnett, 1965). For the Tory IIA reactor tests the site housed 120,000 lb. of air stored at 3000-4000 psi and 1,200,000 lb. of air at a similar psi for the Tory IIC reactor tests (PNPC, 1962).

The Tory-IIA reactor was test run several times at the LRL NTS during 1961. The Tory-IIA tests runs were limited, known as partial-scale tests, but they provided valuable data on various research areas, such as 'fuel element integrity under realistic

16

operating conditions' (Goldberg, 1962). The most important aspect point established from the Tory-IIA tests was that they proved that a reactor for the ramjet engine concept was feasible from an engineering standpoint. The reactor had shown its ability to withstand the very high temperatures and high power output for the specified run time (Goldberg, 1962). The Tory-IIA phase was operated under its design limits on 5 October 1961 (VHC).

This photograph apparently depicts the Tory IIA reactor employed for reduced-scale test runs.

The Tory-IIC test phase was intended to be a full-scale ground-based reactor test series for a ramjet nuclear reactor that would lead to a design for incorporation in a prototype air vehicle. This meant that, unlike the partial test phase of the Tory-IIA, the Tory-IIC reactor had to be designed complete with the associated 'control element' problems (Goldberg, 1962). Pre-test, the intention was to run the Tory-IIC reactor at full power, stated as 500 MW (Megawatt) (VHC). This was similar to values being studied in the USSR, stated as 490 MW (Nesterenko *et al*, 1957) for a potential Soviet air vehicle powered by a nuclear ramjet. Peak fuel element temperatures were expected to reach 2500° F (Fahrenheit) for a run time of 5 minutes (Goldberg, 1962). The power output specified for a production reactor to propel the ramjet planned for the Chance Vought SLAM was 600 MW (VHC).

The Tory IIC test reactor was to be fueled by ceramic BO (Beryllium Oxide) of high temperature, which was mixed with enriched UO^2 (Uranium Oxide) and, in small quantity, ZrO^2 (Zirconium dioxide) – this latter material was added to make the mixture more stable. The fuel mixture was put through high pressure process at a facility of the Coors Porcelain Company before it was sintered (VHC) – a process whereby a substance, such as powdery material, is formed into a solid mass through exposure to intense heat, without melting the material. The various fuel elements were formed into hollowed out hexagonal tube structures that measured around 4 in

(10.16 cm), length, by 0.3 in (~0.76 cm), width across flats of hexagon, with an internal (hollowed) diameter of 0.227 in (~0.576 cm). Storing of the fuel rods was end to end, for a total combined length of 50.7 in (~128.78 cm) for the passage of heated air. In total 27,000 heated air channels and 465,000 fuel elements were incorporated (VHC).

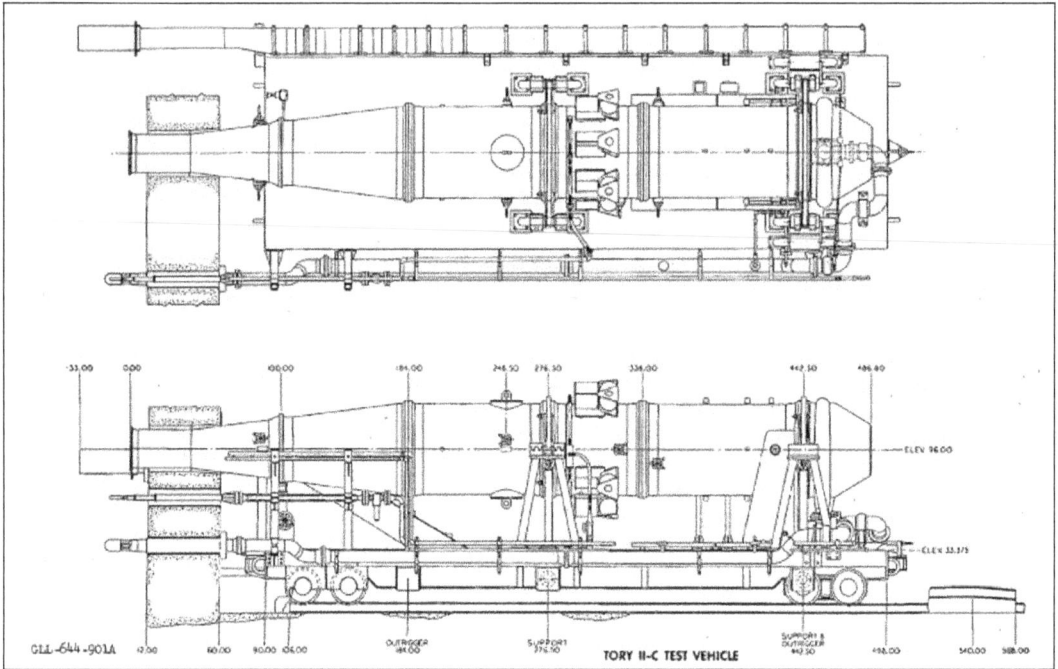

Diagram of the Tory IIC ground based nuclear reactor employed to demonstrate the full-scale run on 20 May 1964. Taken from Barnett, 1965

There were a number of test phases that led to the full scale test of the Tory IIC reactor on 20 May 1964. The first of these was the facility qualification phase, which commenced on 17 November 1962 and lasted until 5 March that year. This phase covered four major areas – air supply cleanup testing, qualification tests of the facility components, qualification tests of the test vehicle (Tory IIC reactor) and training of the operators. The test vehicle qualification tests were conducted in the late stages of the facility qualification phase. The test vehicle itself was basically a 'railroad flatcar', which accommodated the 'ducting that contained the reactor core and control rod actuators' (Barnett, 1965). During these tests, which included a number of blowdowns and several electronic simulation runs to provide data on reactor behavior, some deficiencies were uncovered, particularly during the blowdowns. Among the most serious was the discovery of higher than expected 'temperature connector faults in control rod actuator packages, insufficient nozzle cooling flow' and the requirement for alteration of the design of the mounting for the pressure and temperature probe (Barnett, 1965).

Following transfer of the Tory IIC reactor to the NTS the supercritical experiment phase was conducted on 23 March 1964. The main aim of this phase was the verification that, following insertion of all of the reactors operational fuel rods, these could all be withdrawn again without having a negative effect of an unacceptably high increase in multiplication, an event that could be dangerous. An acceptable level of multiplication, established through experiments that had been conducted at LRL, was put at M ≈ 15 (approximately equal). This value was relevant for a scenario whereby all operational rods were withdrawn, the 6 L (innermost available radius)-ring rods were inserted and the 12 N-ring rods, which were inserted by hand, were in place (Barnett, 1965).

The Cold Critical experiment phase was conducted on 24 March 1964, the day after the supercritical experiment. This paved the way for moving on to hot zero power tests, which were conducted on 9 and 23 April 1964. A hot low power test was conducted on 7 May 1964, followed by an intermediate power test on 12 May that year. This test was significant because the reactor was, for the first time, run at a significant power setting. The run simulated conditions of Mach 2.8 flight speed at an altitude of 10,000 ft. (3048 m). The 12 May test paved the way for the full-scale test run conducted on 20 May 1964, which simulated flight conditions of Mach 2.8 at sea level, with environmental conditions of 10° Fahrenheit. In this phase the reactor was run for a duration of 292 seconds as this was the limit of operation before the air supply within the storage area – this contained 1.2 million lb. of air, noted above – was exhausted. The air supply was heated to a temperature of 943° Fahrenheit and forced through at a pressure setting of 316 psi, required to provide an acceptable simulation of the conditions of the ramjet diffuser (VHC).

The Tory IIA reduced scale and Tory IIC full scale reactor tests verified that the nuclear ramjet concept for the SLAM missile was viable. It was estimated that a serial reactor would produce a neutron flux of 7 x 10^{14} N/CM^2 in the vehicle forward section and 9 x 10^{17} N/CM^2 in the vehicle aft section. Gamma Ray energy output was estimated to be in the region of 1.2 x 10^8 MEV in the vehicle electronics bay and in the region of 4 x 10^{11} MEV in the vehicle aft section (VHC).

Flight Mach number	2.8	3.0	2.8
Flight altitude, ft.	1,000	1,000	1,000
Ambient temperature, ° F	100	100	100
Reactor inlet total temperature, ° F	946	1063	600
Total reactor inlet pressure, psia	322	349	325
Reactor and power, MW (Megawatt)	513	512	633
Reactor flow rate, pps	1,738	1,854	1,852
Net base thrust, lb.	40,000	33,726	61,300
Max fuel element wall temp, ° F	2500	2500	2500
Max fuel element thermal stress, psi	17,500	17,600	21,700
Max element material power density, MW/ft.^{3}	24.24	24.20	29.91

Table 2. Performance characteristics for Tory IIC test reactor at March 1962. Data taken from Var *et al*, 1962

This image appears to show work carried out on elements of the SLAM design on a test stand. It is unclear to what scale these elements were constructed. VHC

SLAM VEHICLE

There were piloted airframes designed for Mach 3 flight at high altitudes developed in the period of the late 1950's through 1964, including the Lockheed A-12 and North American XB-70. No such airframes had been designed for flight close to Mach 3 in the considerably more challenging environment of sea level in the Troposphere (the Troposphere starts at sea level and extends to altitudes of between 8 and 14.5 km (5-9 miles), beyond which lies the Stratosphere (NASA). In such an environment the aircraft outer skin would be expected to heat to temperatures of around 1,000° Fahrenheit and sound pressure levels would be expected to reach around 162 db. (VHC).

To cope with the extremely high skin surface temperatures that would be encountered in a multi-Mach low altitude flight environment, an extensive research/investigation effort was conducted to provision a suitable material able to withstand such high temperatures. This resulted in the Rene 41 stainless steel being selected and fabricated for selected areas of the SLAM (Supersonic Low Altitude Missile) fuselage surface – skin thickness ranging from 1/10 to 1/4 of an inch. Rene 41 had undergone a program of strength testing, a furnace being employed to replicate the temperatures of 1,000° Fahrenheit that would be encountered in a flight regime of around 500 ft. to 1,000 ft. altitude, approaching a speed of Mach 3. The problem of heat generated through radiation was to be solved through gold plating the most affected areas of the forward fuselage, which would dissipate the heat rather than have it concentrated (VHC).

During the SLAM concept development phase close to 1,600 hours of wind-tunnel tests were conducted throughout all of the US government funded national laboratories. For optimum operation in the challenging flight environment of multi-Mach speed in the lower Troposphere, Chance Vought settled on a winged configuration with small canard fore-planes. Wind tunnel tests were also conducted on a 1/3-scale model of the nose, inlet and duct sections (VHC).

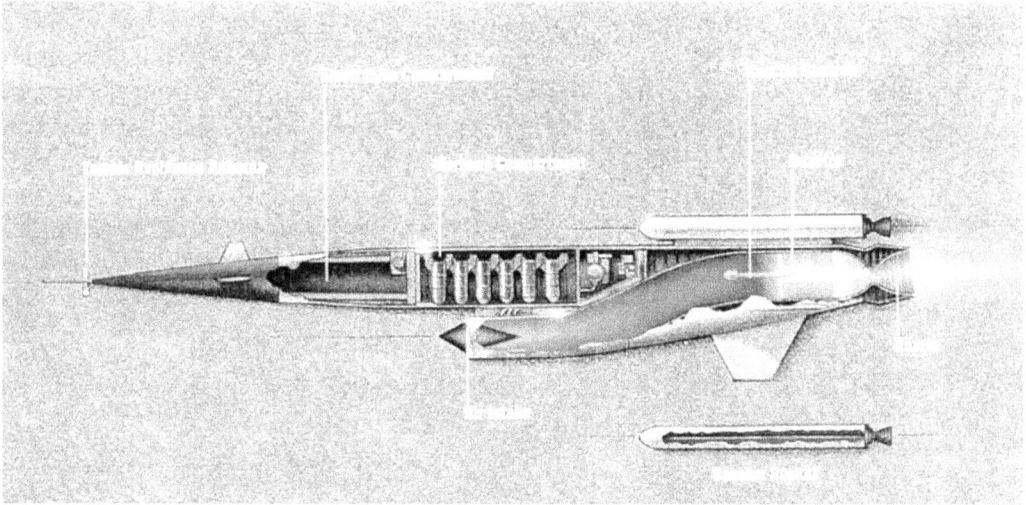

Diagram showing the main sections of the SLAM vehicle and the disposable chemical fueled boosters. Note that the weapon carriage is depicted here as what appears to be six rows of two 1 megaton nuclear bombs, whereas most documentation refers to a weapon load of 16 such bombs. VHC

The major sections of the SLAM vehicle consisted of, from fore to aft: terrain avoidance antenna; terrain avoidance complex; electronics compartment; warhead compartment, containing up to 16 x 1 MT (Megaton) yield nuclear bombs; air intake section below the warhead compartment; reactor control section; nuclear reactor and exhaust exit nozzle with the chemical fuel booster rockets attached to the airframe above the reactor control and reactor sections. The major control surfaces consisted of a moderate 'Y' or tri-fin configuration toward the rear of the fuselage, just forward of the nozzle section. The two upper fins were angled at around 45° (based on visual calculation from test models of the SLAM vehicle), whilst the single lower fin was in the direct downward position. By contrast the two small canard fore-planes were in the 90° horizontal with the single small upper fin in the vertical attitude. The forward control surfaces were located in the nose section, just forward of the electronics compartment. Air would be fed to the nuclear ramjet engine through a pitch/yaw scoop air intake design, which was selected over the classic spike inlet design. Able to operate over a larger performance area, the scoop design was endowed with a pressure recovery of 86%, which, it is stated, 'exceeded program goals' (VHC), although the value for the program goals was not provided.

The decision to forgo shielding against radiation generated by the nuclear reactor posed problem in determining the electronics suite for the SLAM complex. These systems would have to operate in a harsh radiation environment and be capable of surviving in operable condition for the several hours that would have been required for the SLAM to reach its targets in the heart of the Soviet Union. To achieve the limited operational life required, industry was tasked with developing systems with limited insulation, this feeding into the electronics suite, guidance system, control and telemetry systems. This involved what was then the most intensive US radiation testing, which was, conducted in 1964 at the USAF NARF (Nuclear Aircraft Research Facility) at Plant 4 within the Convair Division of General Dynamics (RMANPP AEC, 1963 and VHC). These radiation tests indicated that the electronics were capable of achieving the few hours lifespan required to accomplish the mission from launch to target impact (VHC).

A 1/10 Scale model of the Chance Vought SLAM concept. VHC

The warhead design was undetermined at the time of cancellation. The B53 developed for carriage by the B-47 and B-52 inhabited bombers, from 1962, would have been somewhat large for carriage in the SLAM vehicle. The smaller, 1 MT yield weapons planned may well have emerged as a reduced size weapon based on the B53 design, which was parachute retarded on its descent, a requirement for the weapon to be released from SLAM considering the low altitude release, despite the multi-Mach speed.

Unlike a single warhead missile that had a single target point, the SLAM concept called for a guidance system able to navigate to several targets, each of which would be bombed in turn. To accomplish this would require what was referred to as a dual guidance system, the design of which incorporated what was referred to as gas dynamic bearings for the complexes gyroscopes – specifically developed for the SLAM complex and related nuclear powered aviation programs. As noted above, the components of the system, which had to be hardened against the adverse effects of radiation, prevalent in a design that forwent reactor shielding, to allow the operating life of several hours to be achieved, were tested in the USAF NARF facility. The various tests of the guidance system concept confirmed that the system would allow for completion of the SLAM mission profile through a series of mid-course corrections and a terminal phase course correction (VHC).

Artist depiction of a SLAM vehicle on the low-level part of its flight to the target area. VHC

Chance Vought funded studies for mission systems that could be employed in the SLAM concept. This would lead to a system referred as FINGERPRINT, but latter changed to TERCOM (Terrain Contour Matching) after the rights for the program were handed over to the USAF (VHC). TERCOM employed a procedure in which terrain contours along the missile flight path would be loaded into a digital database, effectively a matrix which would relate to data or numbers that were sequentially arranged. Although not as accurate as today's highly detailed maps obtained from modern satellites mapping, the contours available in maps of Earth's land masses in the early 1960's allowed natural elevations to be taken into account in determining the missile's flight path. This would be particularly important in the terminal phase of the flight, which would be conducted at altitudes of 1,000 ft. down to 500 ft. The elevation data stored in the TERCOM database would then be compared with that of data received from downward looking radar as the missile overflew a particular point of the Earth's surface. This would allow corrections to the missile flight path to the target to be made, as required. This procedure could be conducted several times, allowing the SLAM vehicle to navigate routes to up to 16 separate targets as required. The suitability of TERCOM for the SLAM mission was verified by a number of system tests in testbed platforms, conducted over various types of terrain, including terrain covered by snow (VHC).

TERCOM formed the cornerstone of the guidance systems of US surface launched cruise missiles of the late Cold War period, continuing, in more advanced form, into the twenty first century (VHC).

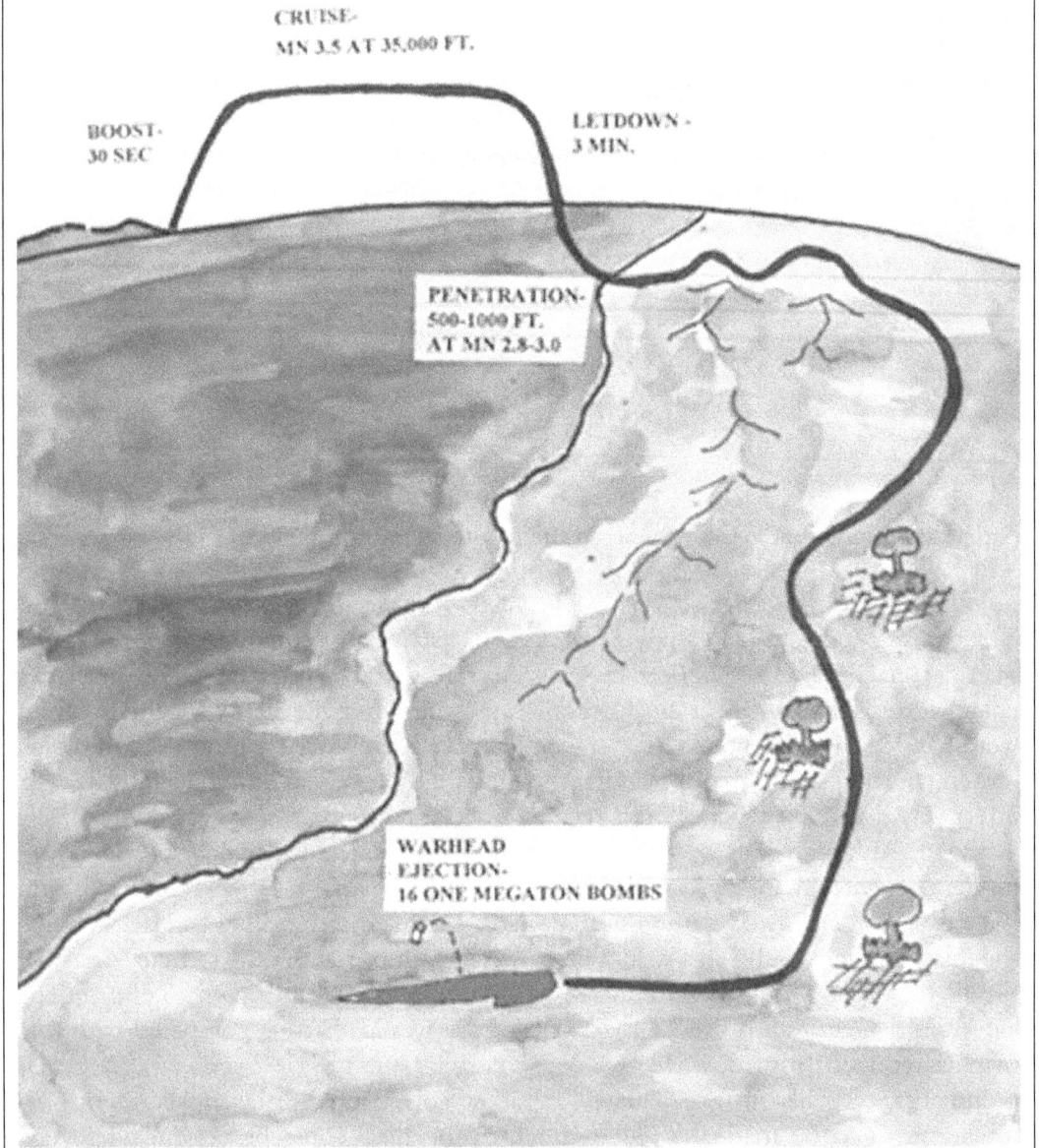

Diagram outlining the basic mission profile for the SLAM concept. VHC

Whereas the SM-62 had been designed to operate at altitudes above 70,000 ft. the SLAM was designed to operate at lower altitudes, particularly in the penetration and terminal phases of the flight. This would be an attempt to overcome the threat posed to high flying air vehicles by Soviet surface to air missile technology, which was making great strides forward at the time of the SLAM vehicle development.

The basic SLAM mission profile would have commenced with launch from a surface launch complex, followed by a 30 second booster phase, taking the missile to 35,000 ft. (10668 m) altitude where the ramjet, propelled by the nuclear reactor, took over for the cruise flight, which would reach up to Mach 3.5 speed after the booster rockets had been jettisoned. When nearing defended airspace the missile descended, at a speed of Mach 3.0, to an altitude of 1000- 500 ft. (~305-152 m) to commence the penetration phase, which was conducted at a speed of Mach 2.8-3.0. Following a profile that aimed to avoid very high terrain the missile would navigate to a preset number of targets, which were bombed with free fall nuclear bombs of a yield of 1 MT.

Diameter: 5 ft. (1.524 m)
Length: 65 ft. (19.812 m)
Weight: 45,000 lb. (20411.55 kg)
Propulsion: 600 Megawatt generated by nuclear reactor (one of half of the power output of Boulder Dam, Colorado, at that time)
Range: Theoretically unlimited (Global)
Speed: Mach 3 or 2,280 mph (3669.304 km/h)
Guidance: Inertial + TERCOM (TERCOM was developed specifically for the SLAM program)
Warheads: up to 16 x 1 megaton bombs
Lift/Drag ratio: 2/1
Missile skin temperature in cruise flight: 1,000° Fahrenheit
Airframe material: Rene 41 Stainless Steel – Gold Plated for radiation cooling
Skin thickness: 1/10 to 1/4 inch
Flight profile: Launch from mobile or stationary launcher by 3 solid propellant booster rockets to a high-altitude cruise, then a descent to altitudes of 1000-500 ft. (305-152 m) for Mach 3 penetration to the target area(s) for ejection of up to 16 one megaton hydrogen bombs over separate targets

Table 3. SLAM Specification – data furnished by Vought History Centre

The SLAM design concept studies, which continued until mid-1964, combined with the testing of the Tory IIA/C nuclear reactor to demonstrate the viability of nuclear propulsion to power the missile, indicated that the concept of a nuclear powered cruise missile with global range was technically feasible (VHC) from an engineering standpoint. However, by this time the concept had been overtaken by the huge strides made in in ICBM development – the ICBM proving to have more promise as a strategic strike weapon than a multi-Mach cruise missile. SLAM's great disadvantages over the ICBM were several fold. It required more maintenance, more ground support infrastructure and personnel – it took the best part of a day to prepare for launch, making it more vulnerable to a first strike – and it was more vulnerable to enemy defensive countermeasures and took considerably longer to reach its target(s). These disadvantages outweighed the major advantage SLAM had over the early ICBM'S, its payload carrying ability – 16 warheads, which was considerably more than the single warhead of first generation ICBM's and the multiple warhead capability planned for next generation ICBM's.

The manned strategic bomber had a number of advantages over the SLAM concept, including heavier payload, a degree of call-back ability, the ability to be on airborne alert or ground alert, removing and reducing respectively the chance of being caught on the ground in a Soviet first strike and the ability to be tasked and re-tasked for a variety of operational scenario's, conventional and nuclear strike. SLAM had a number of advantages over the manned strategic bomber, not least of which was its higher speed and, therefore, faster warhead delivery, and its unlimited range. This latter point would have been negated had a strategic bomber with a nuclear power plant been developed through to fruition. Such a manned aircraft would have had the advantage of non-deliberate loss of the reactor fissionable material, but would have been more vulnerable to Soviet air defenses. The most prominent disadvantage of the manned nuclear powered strategic bomber would have been the prohibitive costs, which would have dwarfed those of the SLAM concept due to the significantly larger size and the need to provide shielding for the crew from the effects of radiation from the reactor.

A not inconsiderable detrimental effect on the environment was inherent in the fact that the operation of the SLAM concept involved the depositing of radioactive fissionable material into the atmosphere during its flight. The environmental damage that such ejection of fissionable material into the atmosphere would cause, along with the ultimate disposal of fissionable material at the end of the mission, affected the planning for flight testing of the SLAM concept. It was concluded that such test flights would be conducted over the North West Pacific Ocean, with the test flights ending with decent of the vehicle into the ocean in the areas used to conduct the US atmospheric nuclear warhead tests (VHC). As the damaging effects of fissionable material was being better understood it was becoming clear that such a concept as SLAM, which would have to undergo considerable flight testing, was unacceptable due to the damage it would cause to the atmospheric and oceanic environment in whatever region the flight was conducted over. The disadvantages, in comparison to other methods of warhead delivery, noted above, and environmental damage issues of the SLAM program, led to its cancellation, the US Department of Defence and US State Department formally notifying Chance Vought of its decision in July 1964. Among the reasons cited was the case forwarded that if such a weapon system entered service with the US then the Soviet Union would be compelled to develop such a system for their own use. However, the Soviets had pioneered the introduction of the ICBM and SLBM (Submarine Launched Ballistic Missile) in the late 1950's and was committed to building up respective forces of such weapons as the main elements of her nuclear deterrent forces. In this respect the Soviet's had cancelled plans for chemical fueled and nuclear powered intercontinental range cruise missiles several years before the United States cancellation of SLAM – the ICBM and SLBM remaining the cornerstone of NATO and Russian Federation nuclear deterrence in the second decade of the twenty first century.

Ultimately multi-Mach cruise missile concepts lost out in the development pathway to ICBM's, which had been heralded in in the late 1950's – the Soviet R-7 (above), had, in August 1957, become the first successfully launched ICBM design. MODRF

GLOSSARY

AEC	Atomic Energy Commission
ANP	Aircraft Nuclear Propulsion
ANPO	Aircraft Nuclear Propulsion Office
ANPP	Aircraft Nuclear Propulsion Project
BO	Beryllium Oxide
CAMAL	Continuous Airborne Missile Launcher and Low Level Weapon
CAML	Continuously Airborne Missile Launcher
Chance Vought	From 1954, Chance Vought Aeronautics Inc., changed to Chance Vought Corporation from 31 December 1960
Convair	Consolidated Vultee
CS	Characteristic Summary
db.	Decibel
DoD	Department of Defense
F	Fahrenheit
ft.	Feet (united of measurement)
GE	General Electric
ICBM	Intercontinental Ballistic Missile
kg	Kilogram
km	Kilometer
km/h	Kilometers per hour
lb.	Pound (unit of weight)
LRL	Lawrence Radiation Laboratory
M	Metre
Mach	1 Mach = the speed of sound (this varies with altitude changes in type and temperature of the medium)
Megaton	1 Megaton = 10^6 (1,000.000) tons of TNT
MEV	Mega Electron Volt
Mph	Miles per hour
MW	Megawatt
MW/ft.^{3}	MW per cubic foot
NACA	National Advisory Commission for Aeronautics
NARF	Nuclear Aircraft Research Facility
N/CM^2	Neutrons transiting through an area of 1 centimeter squared per second
NEPA	Nuclear Energy for Propulsion of Aircraft
nm	Nautical miles
NMUSAF	National Museum of the United States Air Force
NTS	Nevada Test Site
P&W	Pratt & Whitney
Psi	Pounds per square inch
RFP	Request for Proposal
SAC	Standard Aircraft Characteristics
SLAM	Supersonic Low Altitude Missile

SLBM	Submarine Launched Ballistic Missile
TERCOM	Terrain Contour Matching
UO^2	Uranium Oxide
US	United States (of America)
USAF	United States Air Force
USSR	Union of Soviet Socialist Republics
VHC	Vought History Centre
X	Experimental
ZrO^2	Zirconium dioxide
°	Degree(s)
° R	Degrees, total temperature
~	Approximately equal (can also be used to mean asymptotically equal)
≈	Approximately equal
10^6	1,000,000 (1 million). Power of ten in mathematics ($10^1 = 10$; $10^6 = 1$ million etc.)

BIBLIOGRAPHY

Barnett, Charles (1965) 'Tory IIC Test Operations', University of California, Lawrence Radiation Laboratory, Livermore, California

Controller General of the United States (1963) 'Review of Manned Aircraft Nuclear Propulsion Program', Atomic Energy Commission and Department of Defense, Washington

Goldberg, Eugene (1962) 'The Tory II-C Program: Introduction and General Description', University of California, Lawrence Radiation Laboratory, Livermore, California

Merkle, Theodore C. (1959) 'The Nuclear Ramjet Propulsion System', University of California, Lawrence Radiation Laboratory, Livermore, California

Nesterenko, G. N., Sobolev, A. L. & Sushkov, Yu. N. (1957) 'Application of Atomic Engines in Aviation', Military Press of the Ministry of Defense of the USSR

Rom, Frank E. (1954) 'Analysis of a Nuclear Powered Ram-Jet Missile', Lewis Flight-Propulsion Laboratory, Cleveland, Ohio

Sams, Eldon W. & Rom, Frank E. (1953) 'Analysis of Low-Temperature Nuclear-Powered Ram-jet Missile For High Altitudes', Lewis Flight-Propulsion Laboratory, Cleveland, Ohio

United States Atomic Energy Commission Division of Technical Information (1962) 'Proceedings of Nuclear Propulsion Conference', Naval Postgraduate School, Monterey, California

Var, R., Uthe, P. M. & Mintz, M. (1962) 'Tory II-C Performance Parameters', University of California, Lawrence Radiation Laboratory, Livermore, California

Characteristic Summary (1952) 'Research X-6', US DoD, August 1952

Characteristic Summary (1952) 'Research X-6', US DoD, November 1952

Characteristic Summary (1960), 'Strategic Missile, SM-62A', US Department of Defense

Characteristic Summary (1963), 'Tactical Missile (RFML), CGM-13B (TM-76A)', US Department of Defense

S-25 Berkut Historical/Technical factsheet, NPO Almaz, Russian Federation

Tempest Historical/Technical factsheet, Laspace, Russian Federation

TM-61 Matador factsheet, NMUSAF

TM-76B (CGM-13B (MGM-13) Mace factsheet, NMUSAF

Standard Missile Characteristics (1960), 'SM-62A Snark', Secretary of the Air Force, USAF

Standard Missile Characteristics (1957), 'SM-64A Navaho', Secretary of the Air Force, USAF

Vought History Centre factsheet on the Supersonic Low Altitude Missile

NB-36H Crusader factsheet, NMUSAF

Additional graphic material has been sourced from NASA (National Aeronautics and Space Administration) from archives of NACA (National Advisory Committee for Aeronautics)

ABOUT THE AUTHOR

Hugh Harkins FRAS is a historian and author with an extensive research background in astro/geophysics and studies/research in the wider scientific, aeronautic, astronautic and nautical technical and historical fields. He is also involved in research in the field of Scottish history, which formed a significant element of an otherwise scientific undergraduate degree. Hugh has published in excess of sixty books; non-fiction and fiction, writing under his given name as well as utilising several pseudonyms. He has also written for several international magazines, whilst his work has been used as reference for many other projects ranging from the aviation industry, international news corporations and film media to encyclopaedias, museum exhibits and the computer gaming industry. Hugh is a member of the Institute of Physics and is an elected Fellow of the Royal Astronomical Society. He currently resides in his native Scotland. Other titles by the author include:

XF-103 - Mach 3 Stratospheric Interceptor Concept
North American F-108 Rapier - Mach 3 Interceptor
Convair YB-60 - Fort Worth Overcast
K-15/M System - Soviet Supersonic All-Weather Interceptor Complex
Soviet Mixed Power Experimental Fighter Aircraft - Piston-Liquid Propellant Rocket Engine/Piston-Ramjet/Piston-Pulsejet & Piston-Compressor Jet Engine Designs of the 1940's
Boeing X-36 Tailless Agility Flight Research Aircraft
X-32 - The Boeing Joint Strike Fighter
X-35 - Progenitor to the F-35 Lightning II
X-45 Uninhabited Combat Air Vehicle
Orbital/Fractional Orbit Bombardment System - The Soviet Globalnaya Raketa
Counter-Space Defence Co-Orbital Satellite Fighter
Russia's Coastal Missile Shield - Bal-E & Bastion Mobile Coastal Cruise Missile Complexes
Iskander - Mobile Tactical Aero-Ballistic/Cruise Missile Complex
Russia's Strategic Missile Carrier/Bomber Roadmap 2018-2040 – PAK DA, Tu-160M2, Tu-95MSM & Tu-22M3M
Sukhoi T-50/PAK FA - Russia's 5th Generation 'Stealth' Fighter
Sukhoi Su-35S 'Flanker' E - Russia's 4++ Generation Super-Manoeuvrability Fighter
Sukhoi Su-34 'Fullback'
Sukhoi Su-30MKK/MK2/M2 - Russo Kitashiy Striker from Amur
MiG-35/D 'Fulcrum' F – Towards the Fifth Generation
Air War over Syria, Tu-160, Tu-95MS & Tu-22M3 - Cruise Missile and Bombing Strikes on Syria, November 2015-February 2016
Sukhoi Su-27SM(3)/SKM
Russian/Soviet Aircraft Carrier & Carrier Aviation Design & Evolution Volume 1 - Seaplane Carriers, Project 71/72, Graf Zeppelin, Project 1123 ASW Cruiser & Project 1143-1143.4 Heavy Aircraft Carrying Cruiser
Light Battle Cruisers and the Second Battle of Heligoland Bight
British Battlecruisers of World War 1 - Operational Log, July 1914-June 1915
Eurofighter Typhoon - Storm over Europe
Into The Cauldron - The Lancaster MK.I Daylight Raid on Augsburg
Hurricane IIB Combat Log - 151 Wing RAF, North Russia 1941
RAF Meteor Jet Fighters in World War II, an Operational Log
Typhoon IA/B Combat Log - Operation Jubilee, August 1942
Defiant MK.I Combat Log - Fighter Command, May-September 1940
Blenheim MK.IF Combat Log - Fighter Command Day Fighter Sweeps/Night Interceptions, September 1939 - June 1940